PRE TEEN PRESSURES

CHILD ABUSE

by Debra Goldentyer

RSVP

RAINTREE STECK-VAUGHN
PUBLISHERS
The Steck-Vaughn Company

Austin, Texas

Consultants
Beverly Arneth, Director of the Family Preservation Program, Family Guidance Center, Trenton, NJ
William B. Presnell, Clinical Member, American Association for Marriage and Family Therapy

Developed for Steck-Vaughn Company by
Visual Education Corporation, Princeton, New Jersey
Project Director: Jewel Moulthrop
Editor: Paula McGuire
Editorial Assistant: Jacqueline Morais
Photo Research: Sara Matthews
Electronic Preparation: Cynthia C. Feldner, Manager; Fiona Torphy
Production Supervisor: Ellen Foos
Electronic Production: Lisa Evans-Skopas, Manager; Elise Dodeles, Deirdre Sheean, Isabelle Verret
Interior Design: Maxson Crandall

Raintree Steck-Vaughn Publishers staff
Editor: Kathy DeVico
Project Manager: Joyce Spicer

Photo Credits: Cover: © Tony Freeman/PhotoEdit; 9: © Tony Freeman/PhotoEdit; 10: © Alan Oddie/PhotoEdit; 14: © David Young-Wolff/PhotoEdit; 18: © Tom Edwards/ Unicorn Stock Photos; 21: © Martin Jones/Unicorn Stock Photos; 28: © David Young-Wolff/PhotoEdit; 35: © Eric R. Berndt/Unicorn Stock Photos; 40: © David Young-Wolff/ PhotoEdit; 41: © Richard Hutchings/PhotoEdit; 44: © Bill Aron/PhotoEdit

Library of Congress Cataloging-in-Publication Data
Goldentyer, Debra, 1960–
    Child abuse/by Debra Goldentyer.
       p.   cm. — (Preteen pressures)
    Includes bibliographical references (p. 47) and index.
    Summary: Discusses how to recognize and deal with different kinds of child abuse, including physical abuse, sexual abuse, and neglect.
    ISBN 0-8172-5032-8
    1. Child abuse—Juvenile literature. 2. Child abuse—United States—Juvenile literature. [1. Child abuse.] I. Title. II. Series.
    HV6626.5.G636 1998
    326.76′0973—dc21

                                         97-27927
                                           CIP
                                            AC

Printed and bound in the United States
1 2 3 4 5 6 7 8 9 0 LB 01 00 99 98 97

CONTENTS

INTRODUCTION

I t's often a big secret. A parent or guardian is supposed to be a child's protector and best friend. But it doesn't always happen that way. Instead, the adult is hitting the child, scaring the child, or ignoring the child's needs. Over six million children are abused and neglected in this country every year. Hundreds die each year from this abuse and neglect. Every 13 seconds a child is attacked—by a parent, a stepparent, a guardian, an older brother or sister, another relative, or a family friend.

It's often a big secret, but it's not a good secret to keep. Many children who are abused don't tell anyone. It's difficult to understand why someone they know and care about would hurt them. Some children feel too ashamed to talk about it. Some think that the abuse is their fault. Some think they deserve the bad treatment. Some children are afraid to make trouble for the abuser, because they fear greater abuse if they tell. Many abused children work hard to cover their injuries. They lie to protect their abusers, and they cry on the way home from school each day. Home for these children is not a safe place, and they feel helpless to change the situation.

Abuse can be stopped, but not until someone else knows that it's happening. What can be done if you or someone you know is being abused? Reading this book will give you important information that can help to end the bad treatment. We will discuss the causes and effects of abuse. We will suggest places where you can go for help.

Most of all we hope that after you read this book, you will have the information you need—and the courage—to speak up. With counseling and treatment, most abusers can learn to change their behavior. By telling someone, you can end the abuse and help both the abuser and the victim.

Statistics About Abuse, 1994

Frequency of attacks on children	Every 13 seconds
Estimated number of children who died as a result of abuse or neglect	1,271
Number who die each day	2–5
Percentage of those children who were under age five	88
Number of children permanently disabled as a result of abuse or neglect	18,000
Percentage of child fatalities involving parental substance abuse	29
Number of children suffering from physical neglect	8 in 1,000
Average age of a sexually abused child	10 years old

The estimated number of children for whom reports of child abuse and neglect were made and proven to be valid in the United States in 1994 is 2,036,000.

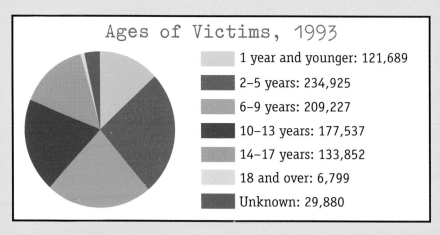

Ages of Victims, 1993

- 1 year and younger: 121,689
- 2–5 years: 234,925
- 6–9 years: 209,227
- 10–13 years: 177,537
- 14–17 years: 133,852
- 18 and over: 6,799
- Unknown: 29,880

Children of all ages have been victims of abuse.

FAMILIES AND CHILD ABUSE

Tuesday, July 30: The call came in at 8:03 P.M. Officers Kaminsky and Yee arrived at 146 Pine Street in Oakdale at 8:30 P.M. Sarah Peral ran out of the house as soon as the patrol car drove up. She told the officers that her husband, Mark, had beaten their nine-year-old son, Tommy. She could not make him stop. The officers entered the house. The boy was hiding in the closet. He appeared uninjured but scared. Mr. Peral was sitting in the kitchen. When asked what happened, he said, "I can't believe what I've done. I've been under a lot of stress lately. I really messed up this time."

TYPES OF ABUSE

Abuse within a family isn't limited to a parent hitting a child. There are other types of abuse—both physical and emotional.

Physical Abuse

What is physical abuse? Shaking. Slapping. Biting. Burning. Pushing. Punching. Whatever the form, a person—especially a child—does not deserve abuse. Abuse is never the victim's fault. Pete was a victim of physical abuse. His father had a very quick temper. Whenever Pete did anything that made his father angry, his father hit him. Even though Pete was only five years old, his father used all his strength when he hit the boy. One time he slapped Pete so hard that Pete fell backward and rolled down the stairs. Another time Pete's father slammed him into a wall. When Pete hit the wall, a large painting fell on his head.

Physical abuse often leads to broken bones and bruises. It can also cause serious injuries, such as brain damage or some other permanent disability. Sometimes physical abuse leads to death.

Some children are hit or slapped regularly for years. Psychologists have found that these children often suffer from long-term emotional damage. They have very little respect for themselves. That lack of self-respect can last their entire lives—even when they're adults. Many people who have been victims of physical abuse find it difficult to trust other people.

Sexual Abuse

What is sexual abuse? Touching a child in a sexual way. Forcing a child to participate in sexual activities. Bribing, coaxing, asking, or tricking a child into acting in a sexual way. These are examples of sexual abuse.

Ryan was a victim of sexual abuse. His uncle used to baby-sit Ryan on Saturday evenings so that his parents could go out. When they were alone, Ryan's uncle would touch Ryan on the private parts of his body and show him pictures of naked men. Ryan was too young to understand why his uncle made him feel uncomfortable.

Verbal Abuse

What is verbal abuse? It's hearing harsh, negative words like, "Hurry up, you miserable brat!" "Shut up!" "Get out of my sight!" over and over again.

Melanie was a victim of verbal abuse. Her father yelled at her every day. He had no control over his temper. Although he did not hit her, he constantly battered her with words. She was fearful of being around him and awaited his arrival home from work with anxiety. Nobody came to her rescue, and it became clear to Melanie that the whole family was afraid of her father. Melanie became nervous and forgetful. She lost her appetite and began to lose weight.

For a child who is emotionally abused, the psychological scars can be just as painful as physical ones.

Humiliation

What is humiliation? It is teasing, belittling, or embarrassing someone. And it hurts.

Ricky was a victim of humiliation. He had a speech problem that made him stutter. Rather than help him overcome the problem, his parents teased him about the way he spoke. At home they would mock him and interrupt him when he had trouble completing a word. When Ricky's friends came over, his parents would tell them to ignore Ricky's funny way of talking. They told his friends that Ricky talked that way because he was stupid. Ricky learned never to invite friends over to the house.

Physical Neglect

What is physical neglect? Not feeding a child. Not dressing a child warmly. Not washing a child. Ignoring a child's medical needs.

Abuse includes not only what is done to a child, but also what is not done for a child.

Susanna was a victim of child neglect. When she was six years old, her parents decided to go away for the weekend—without Susanna. They left crackers and juice for her, but she had no adult looking after her for three days. She had no one to call if she became sick or injured, or even if she had trouble sleeping. She didn't know how to dress herself. She couldn't adjust the temperature of the house. She didn't wash herself the entire weekend.

Emotional Neglect

What is emotional neglect? Not hugging a child. Not spending time with a child. Ignoring a child.

Joyce was a victim of emotional neglect. Her mother paid no attention to her. She showed Joyce no love or affection. She never asked Joyce about schoolwork or her friends. She never gave Joyce a hug or a kiss.

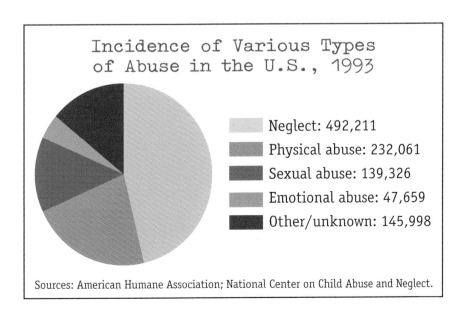

Incidence of Various Types of Abuse in the U.S., 1993

Neglect: 492,211
Physical abuse: 232,061
Sexual abuse: 139,326
Emotional abuse: 47,659
Other/unknown: 145,998

Sources: American Humane Association; National Center on Child Abuse and Neglect.

It's not always easy to tell when a parent or guardian is being abusive or neglectful. Think about these families:

▶ Bonnie is ten years old. She knows that she has to be home from school before three o'clock. She comes in at six o'clock one evening and says that she went to visit a friend and lost track of the time. Bonnie's mother spanks her. Is that abuse?

▶ Rashad is six years old. He climbs onto the kitchen cabinet for a cookie, although he knows that he's not supposed to have one. His father catches him and burns him with his cigarette to teach him a lesson. Is that abuse?

▶ At the beginning of winter, Patrice asks for a new down-filled coat. Patrice's parents tell her that they can't afford to buy her a new coat. Instead, they tell her that she will have to wear her older sister's hand-me-down wool coat. Patrice complains that wool isn't as warm as down and that she'll freeze waiting for the school bus. Is that neglect?

▶ Jason is nine years old. His parents have an overnight trip planned and can't find a baby-sitter. They decide to leave Jason alone. They show him where the cereal and milk are, give him a list of emergency telephone numbers, and tell him not to go outside. Is that neglect?

WHAT IS AND ISN'T ABUSE

Not everything unpleasant, or "mean," that a parent does to a child is abuse. Parents have to set rules for their children—for the children's safety and protection and so that the children will learn to act responsibly. When children break the rules set by their parents, as Bonnie and Rashad did, it's important that the parents discipline and correct them.

Parents use various methods to discipline their children. Some assign special chores or take away certain privileges. These are actions that children are likely to learn from and remember. Others yell at their children or spank them, as Bonnie's mother did. Yelling and spanking are not the most effective ways of disciplining a child. However, they are not considered abuse unless they are meant to—or do—cause injury.

It's not abuse to correct or discipline a child. Abuse occurs only when the discipline goes out of control. What Rashad's father did, for example, was much too cruel a punishment. A proper punishment for Rashad might have been dinner without dessert or a day with no television. Burning a child is never a reasonable punishment.

WHAT IS AND ISN'T NEGLECT

Neglect can sometimes be even more difficult to identify than abuse. Parents and guardians are responsible for the care of their children. They must provide the children with proper food and clothing. They must make sure that their children receive the proper medical care, education, and supervision. If they don't, these adults are guilty of child neglect. This is true whether the adult acted on purpose or by accident.

Appropriate and Inappropriate Punishments

Appropriate punishments

▶ Losing desserts, television, computer games, or telephone for a week

▶ Being grounded at home for a period of time

▶ Having to pay to fix something that is damaged

▶ Doing extra chores for a week

Inappropriate

▶ Being beaten

▶ Being denied food

▶ Being ignored by family members

▶ Being burned, cut, or physically injured in any way

▶ Being locked in a room

Not all punishments are inappropriate. A parent can discipline a child without resorting to violence.

Are Patrice's and Jason's parents guilty of neglect? Patrice's parents refused to buy her the coat she wanted, but they did give her a coat that is appropriate for winter weather. They are not guilty of neglect. The requirement that parents give children proper food and clothing doesn't mean that a parent must give the child whatever food and clothing the child wants. It means that parents must give the child appropriate food and clothing, given the family's financial situation and other circumstances.

Jason's parents are guilty of neglect. While his parents left him food, they did not leave him under proper supervision. Jason is only nine years old. He is not old enough to stay overnight alone.

OTHER ABUSIVE FAMILY RELATIONSHIPS

When you hear about abuse within a family, you hear mostly about a parent hurting a child. But it's not just parents who abuse children. Children have been abused in their own homes by baby-sitters, stepparents, parents' friends, brothers, sisters, and other relatives. Outside the home, children have been abused by teachers, day-care workers, neighbors, and other adults and older children.

CAUSES OF ABUSE AND NEGLECT

Len is an adult, but he remembers his childhood very well. He grew up with an abusive father. Here's what he says his childhood was like:

66 I thought my home was normal. It was the only home I knew anything about. It was normal to me that my dad beat me. He beat me at least once a week. I didn't like it, but I didn't know that it was wrong. I didn't know back then that other children aren't beaten by their parents.

My father probably just thought that he was disciplining me, and I thought so, too. I mean, I was a child. I figured, if he's hitting me, he had to hit me. I must have done something wrong. He was my father. He was supposed to love me and care for me. It never occurred to me that he would do anything just to be mean to me or hurt me.

My mother sometimes tried to stop him. But that would make things worse. If she got in his way, my father would hit her, too. I didn't want him to hit her, so I hoped she wouldn't see me getting hit. I used to hide my bruises from her. And of course I never told anyone else about the hitting. I never told my friends or my teachers or anyone. Like I said, I thought my life was normal. **"**

WHO ABUSES?

Parker's grandmother burns him with her cigarettes. Yasmin's father beats her. Catherine's baby-sitter takes her out of the crib and shakes her to make her stop crying. Edwina's uncle touches her in a sexual way. What these children have in common is abuse. But they don't have much else in common:

▶ Parker and Edwina come from rich families; Catherine's family is very poor.

▶ Catherine is Hispanic. Parker's family is Irish American. Yasmin is African American. Edwina is Asian American.

▶ Parker lives in New York City. Yasmin lives in rural Georgia. Catherine lives in a small town in Vermont.

▶ Edwina lives with her uncle and aunt. Catherine lives with both parents. Yasmin lives with just her father.

Abuse happens in all types of families, in all areas of the country, and in families that are small and large, rich and poor, immigrant and native. Abusers don't look any different from anyone else. You can't tell who is an abuser by looking at him or her. If a friend says

Abuse can threaten the security of all types of families.

that a parent or another adult is abusing him or her, take it seriously. It may be hard for you to think that "such a nice person" or "someone from a family just like mine" could be hurting someone he or she loves, but it could very well be true.

THE CAUSES OF ABUSE

People who abuse children—like Parker's grandmother, Yasmin's father, Catherine's baby-sitter, and Edwina's uncle—abuse them for reasons that have nothing to do with the child. It may be that the abuser has an emotional problem. It may be that the abuser is angry at someone else. In many cases, the child simply happened to be in the wrong place at the wrong time.

STRESS

How do you feel when something happens that makes you angry? Do you ever feel like you want to hit something or somebody? This is a common reaction to stress and anger. Some people grab a basketball and shoot hoops to relieve stress. Others take their stress and anger out through other healthy activities, such as dancing, cooking, or long walks. Some people, though, instead of finding a healthy outlet for their stress, take it out on the people around them. They have not learned how to control their negative feelings.

Mrs. Bosson is one of those people. She is a single mother of two children. And she lost her job three months ago. She was very worried about having enough money for her family. She had a job interview to go to Tuesday afternoon, so she asked her 12-year-old son, Andrew, to come home right after school to baby-sit his little sister. Andrew forgot. When Mrs. Bosson came home and found her daughter alone, she became very upset. As soon as Andrew came home, she screamed at him. She hit him. She pushed him down the front steps of their house. Andrew ended up in the hospital. Clearly, a part of why Mrs. Bosson was angry was Andrew's behavior. But the underlying reason for her anger was the stress of being unemployed. Andrew was the target of her attack, but not the real cause of it.

LOW SELF-ESTEEM

Self-esteem is respect for yourself. Some people have low self-esteem. They think that they can't do anything right. They feel unhappy and powerless. Some people suffer from low self-esteem all the time. Others feel this way when circumstances are going poorly for them, such as when they are having trouble at school or at work or when they don't have a job they like.

What do people with low self-esteem do? The smart ones look for ways to feel better about themselves. They may work harder at school or look for a new job. Some go to counselors to learn how to raise their self-esteem. Those who aren't so smart look for easy ways to feel powerful. Unfortunately, some think that they can feel better by attacking someone smaller or weaker than they are, like a child. Hitting a child can give a person with low self-esteem a brief feeling of power or control in a world where that person is feeling out of control.

SUBSTANCE ABUSE

Maddie's father drank a lot. Whenever he was drunk, he smacked her. Maddie learned to hide from him whenever she saw him reaching for his bottles.

People who use alcohol or drugs can have trouble controlling their behavior. Drugs and alcohol lessen people's self-control. Drugs and alcohol reduce a person's ability to think or act reasonably. About one in three cases of child abuse occurs when the abuser has been drinking or using cocaine or other illegal drugs.

Uncontrollable drinking can lead to violent behavior.

IMMATURITY OR LACK OF PARENTING SKILLS

Both of Bobby's parents worked long hours. When Bobby's little sister, Mia, was born, his parents put him in charge of taking care of her. But Bobby was only nine years old, and no one had taught him how to take care of an infant. He would leave Mia out in the hot sun while he played basketball with his friends. He would give her soda to drink instead of milk or juice. He and his friends would sometimes play roughly and toss her back and forth like a toy. Once, when Mia developed a high fever, Bobby tried to make her feel cooler by moving her crib next to an open window. It was a cold winter's day, and Mia's illness became worse.

Many young parents have no more experience than Bobby. They find themselves at home alone with a baby and no family support—and no idea of how to take care of the baby. This can lead to neglect and physical or emotional abuse.

PERSONAL HISTORY

Many adults who abuse children were abused themselves when they were children. Much of what adults know about raising children, they learned from watching their own parents. If their parents were gentle and fair with them, they tend to be gentle and fair with their own children. If their parents hit or otherwise abused them, they tend to do the same to their children. These adults—who are now parents themselves—don't know that they are abusing their children. They have simply learned that hitting is the way to discipline children.

THE CAUSES OF NEGLECT

Abuse is doing something you should not do, such as hitting, burning, or pushing. Neglect is not doing what you should do, such as caring for a child. Parents who neglect their children often do so for the same reasons that other parents abuse their children:

▶ Mrs. Chu was an inexperienced parent. She didn't know that she was supposed to send her children to school or take them for regular medical checkups. She often forgot to change her baby's diaper.

▶ Mrs. Kidder was a drug addict. She rarely took care of herself and nearly always neglected her children. Often her children had nothing to eat but cookies. Once, when she went shopping, she forgot that she'd brought her baby and left the baby in the store.

▶ Mr. Sanders had two jobs and only a half hour between jobs. He used that time to stop by his home, feed his ten-year-old daughter, and put her to bed. Sometimes, if traffic was heavy, he would skip the trip home. He would come home after his night job at three A.M. to find his daughter hungry and asleep in the living room.

SEXUAL ABUSE

Sexual abuse is taking advantage of someone in a sexual way. People of both genders and of all ages may be victims of sexual abuse. Sexual abusers can also be of various ages or of either sex.

FORMS OF SEXUAL ABUSE

Physical Abuse

Rebecca remembers the sexual abuse she suffered: "One of my baby-sitters used to abuse me. When I was littler, he would touch my breasts or reach between my legs. Sometimes he would try to kiss me or hold me tight. It made me uncomfortable, but I didn't know what to do to make him stop."

What Rebecca describes is physical sexual abuse. Most sexual abuse is physical. The abuser may touch or rub a child's genitals, breasts, or other sexual areas or ask the child to touch the abuser in sexual places.

It's important to understand that any sexual activity between an adult and a child is sexual abuse. When the abuser is a member of the child's family, the sexual abuse has a special name: incest.

Nonphysical Abuse

Martin was sexually abused by his grandfather: "My grandfather never touched me, but he still made me very uncomfortable. He would show me magazines and books of men and boys performing sexual acts. Once he brought over a videotape of two men having sex."

Martin's abuse was not in any way physical, but it was still abuse. Like Martin's grandfather, some adults or teens may ask a young person to look at sexual pictures or make them watch sexual acts. This can have a harmful effect on the child's development.

WHY SEXUAL ABUSE HAPPENS

At a counseling center for sexual abusers, several people tried to explain why sexual abuse happens.

Mr. B: I'm in counseling because I abused my son. I had an uncontrollable sexual desire. I like the way little boys look. I like looking at them and touching them. Yes, I know it was wrong, but I couldn't help myself. My son trusted me, and I took advantage of his trust.

Mr. L: I'm 19, and I've sexually abused my little sister since I was 12. Later I found other girls to abuse. I would baby-sit the neighbors' children or visit my sister's friends. I knew it was wrong, but I convinced myself that I wasn't hurting anyone. And I never had sexual intercourse with them. We just played. I think I really believed that the girls enjoyed it.

Ms. W: I abused my son for six years. Until I started seeing my counselor, I truly believed that it was harming no one. I saw it as an expression of love between mother and son. In a way I thought of it as my right, or even my duty, to teach my little boy about sex.

Happily, these sexual abusers have recognized that they need help. While they will receive compassion from their counselors, they also will be given firm treatment. Their behavior is unacceptable and must be stopped.

YOU ARE NOT RESPONSIBLE

The hardest thing for a victim of sexual abuse to understand is that he or she is not responsible for the abuse. This is why many victims of sexual abuse need counseling to help them overcome their feelings about the abuse. Here are some victims' statements that describe their feelings:

Gordon: I was seven years old when my father began abusing me. It was confusing, and it was scary. I knew Dad loved me. I knew that he cared about me. I decided that there must be something wrong with me that I felt so horrible every time Dad touched me in that way.

Rosa: My brother used to tell me he was doing this for me. He said it was his place to teach me what boys want. When I argued with him or told him to stop, he'd say I was ungrateful and I should respect my big brother and thank him for the lessons.

Barbara: My stepfather said I asked for his attention. He said that what he did was my fault: that the way I looked at him was just too hard to resist.

Wendy: My dad started coming into my bed when I was six years old. I knew that I didn't like what he was doing. I asked him to stop, but he wouldn't. Instead he threatened me. He said that if I didn't let him visit me, he'd leave the family. He would divorce my mother. He said it would be my fault. I thought I had no choice but to let him keep visiting.

WHY CHILDREN DON'T TELL

Sexual abusers try to make their victims feel at fault for what happens to them. The victims may feel threatened or ashamed and are unable to stop the abuse or tell anyone it's happening.

Telling someone about the abuse is very difficult to do. In fact, sexual abuse often goes on for a long time, because children say that sometimes it's easier to put up with the abuse than to admit what's been going on. Here's what they say:

▶ I felt like it was my fault. Something I said or something I did suggested that I wanted the attention.

▶ He said it was a good thing, something I should enjoy.

▶ I didn't think anyone would believe me.

▶ I was afraid of what people would say about me.

▶ I was scared of what would happen to him if I told on him.

▶ She threatened to hurt me if I told.

▶ It's been going on too long to tell; people will wonder why I didn't say anything sooner.

Sexually abused children often feel guilty or ashamed of the bad things that older people do to them, but the abuse is never their fault.

▶ I kept hoping he would stop on his own.

▶ She told me no one would believe me.

If you are being sexually abused, it's never too late to bring it to someone's attention. It doesn't matter if the abuse has gone on for three days or three years. You are not responsible for the crime that is being committed.

THE EFFECTS OF SEXUAL ABUSE

Marie's father began sexually abusing her when she was eight years old. He would come into her bedroom at night and touch her in ways that made her very uncomfortable. Marie loved her father, and although she hated these visits, she didn't say anything to anyone about them. This went on for three years, until one day, when Marie was 11 years old, her mother discovered what her father was doing.

Marie's mother divorced her husband, and Marie and her mother moved away. Marie was never abused by her father again. But memories of what had happened affected her for a long time. She felt guilty about not having said anything for so long. She felt ashamed that she had let her father mistreat her. She had nightmares for years.

As Marie became old enough to date, she became even more confused. She liked boys, but she was afraid when they tried to kiss her. She grew ashamed as her body developed. Marie became depressed and withdrawn. She had a muddle of feelings—mostly depression, shame, and guilt. Dealing with them all at once made it hard for her to study or pay attention at school.

Marie's experience is common among children who have been sexually abused. Victims of sexual abuse often confuse sex with love and don't understand their feelings. Marie felt afraid when boys tried to kiss her. Others in the same situation feel guilt so strongly that they lose respect for themselves and openly invite sexual activity with many people.

It can take years of counseling and positive relationships with good men and women, but in time, people who have been sexually abused can learn to feel better about themselves. Marie found this out, and her nightmares went away.

CHANGING THE SITUATION

The first step toward changing your situation is to recognize that you are being abused. The next step is to seek help. This is the hardest step for any abused or neglected child. An abused child has to find a way to speak up. There's not much a child can do alone. A child depends on parents and other adults for many things. A child can't stand up to a parent; move out of the house; or stop depending on the parent for food, shelter, and love. But a child can tell someone what's happening. And the sooner you can do that, the sooner you will find the help you need to make positive changes in your life.

HOW TO TELL SOMEONE

To report child abuse or neglect, you can call one of the toll-free numbers listed at the back of this book. Or you can call a local child welfare hot line. Look in the phone book for:

▶ A child welfare office or a child protective services office

▶ A government health or social services office

▶ The local police

▶ The local hospital

Finding Someone to Talk To

If you are a victim of abuse, you need help. You need to find an adult who can make the abuse stop.

Here are some people you can talk to:

▶ a parent
▶ an uncle, aunt, stepparent, grandparent, or other relative
▶ your older brother or sister
▶ an adult friend
▶ a neighbor
▶ a teacher (it doesn't have to be your teacher)
▶ a school counselor
▶ a local police officer
▶ a doctor
▶ a nurse
▶ a camp counselor
▶ a scout leader
▶ a hot line for children
▶ a friend
▶ the parent of a friend
▶ the older brother or sister of a friend
▶ a priest, minister, or rabbi

If you tell an adult, and he or she does nothing, tell someone else. Keep telling people until someone takes action.

REPORTING LAWS: WATCHING OUT FOR THE CHILDREN

Not only are children afraid to speak up, but neighbors, relatives, and friends often are, too. Often adults who think that something might be wrong are afraid to say anything. They may not want to become involved in what they see as a family matter. Or they feel as if they should wait until they are sure that there is a problem. So the abuse continues. This is why there are now child abuse reporting laws in every state.

HELPING A FRIEND WHO MAY BE ABUSED

What should you do if you think that a friend might be a victim of abuse? That's what Vijay wondered. When he was in sixth grade, he was worried about his classmate Anita. He thought her mother was beating her. He saw some of the signs of abuse. She seemed to get hurt a lot "by accident" at home, her eyes often looked puffy from crying, she seemed scared a lot of the time, and she never wanted to talk about her family.

Here's what Vijay did:

1. He learned what he could about child abuse. He read a few books and collected some pamphlets. He called a child abuse hot line for advice.

2. He asked Anita to take a walk on the beach with him. He wanted to find a place where they could talk without anyone hearing their conversation or interrupting them. He knew that it was important for her to feel safe and comfortable before she talked about this matter.

3. During the walk Vijay told Anita about his concern for her and asked her whether there was a problem at home. She was reluctant to say anything at first.

It took some time and a lot of coaxing. Vijay assured her that he wouldn't tell anyone what she told him. He told her that he was her friend and wanted to help her. Slowly she started telling him that yes, her mother did abuse her. Vijay listened carefully. He didn't say much. He did tell her that none of this was her fault. Then he told her what he'd read about child abuse and what she could do about it.

4. The next day Vijay invited Anita to his house after school. He showed her the brochures he'd collected and left her alone so that she could read them. Figuring that she might be afraid to take the brochures home, he offered to keep them for her at his house.

5. The next time he saw Anita, Vijay stressed how important it was for her to tell an adult about what was going on. She said that she was scared to talk about her mother to anyone else. Vijay offered to go with her to report the abuse. He asked her if she would like to stay at his house for a night or two—just in case. She agreed, and Vijay promised to get his parents' permission.

If you have a friend who you think is being abused, convince him or her to speak up. If that friend refuses to tell anyone, then you should tell someone yourself—perhaps a teacher whom you trust. Be sure also to tell your own parents what's going on. Your friend may be mad at you for telling, but in the end he or she will be much more hurt by the abuse than by your speaking up.

What the Laws Say

If there is reason to believe that a child is being abused or neglected, it must be reported to the proper authority (usually the police, a social welfare agency, or a child welfare agency).

Who the Laws Apply To

In many states the law applies to all adults—not only to people who work professionally with children.

What to Look For

Common Signs of Abuse

▶ Children who have bruises, burns, or broken bones unusually often

▶ Children with bruises around the head or bald patches where hair has been pulled out

▶ Children who wear dark glasses indoors (to hide puffy or black eyes) or long sleeves in warm weather (to hide bruises, burns, or cuts)

▶ Children who refuse to take gym (to avoid taking their clothes off)

▶ Children who refuse to explain their injuries or whose explanations are not believable

▶ Children who seem afraid of adults, who show fear when asked about their home life, or who don't want to go home at the end of the day

Common Signs of Neglect

▶ Children who appear unwashed or who wear torn, dirty, or poorly fitting clothing

▶ Children who appear underfed, underweight, or lacking in energy

▶ Children who wear clothes that are inappropriate for the weather

▶ Children with untreated medical or dental problems

Signs of Abuse that Medical Personnel Look For

▶ Children who frequently show up in the emergency room

▶ Children whose X rays show repeated breaking or twisting of bones

▶ Burns that look as if they were made by cigarettes

▶ Children or parents whose explanations about how the child was hurt don't match the injuries

A doctor may suspect abuse when a child seems to have an unusually high number of accidental injuries.

WHAT HAPPENS WHEN YOU TELL

Anita was pretty scared the day she and Vijay went to the local child welfare office. She'd read the brochures Vijay gave her, but she didn't quite believe that things would work out for the best.

When they arrived, the people there were very nice to them. The receptionist introduced Anita and Vijay to a social worker named Dana Myers.

"Just call me Dana," she told Anita. Then she said, "You have nothing to feel guilty or embarrassed about. You've done a very good, courageous thing by coming here. I've met lots of young people, younger than you, who tell terrible stories about what's happened to them. When I can help them change that, I feel very happy."

Anita felt much better. She thought that Dana really understood what she was going through. Dana seemed to be able to answer Anita's questions before she even asked them.

TELLING THE STORY

First, Dana asked to hear Anita's story. "Anita, I want to make this as easy as possible for you, but I do have some ground rules that I need you to follow. One, it's very important that you be as honest as you can. Don't try to protect your mother or hide anything. Second, don't try to make the story sound worse than it is. Just tell me what's happening."

Anita told Dana her story. Dana asked a lot of questions. She asked Anita about her father and mother and whether she had any brothers or sisters who might also be abused. She asked how long the abuse had been going on. She also asked whether Anita had ever been seriously hurt by her mother.

PROTECTING THE VICTIM

Dana then asked Anita if she thought she was in any immediate danger. If she was afraid of her mother, Dana explained, the agency could come in right away and have her move out of the house—at least for a while. Anita said that she could stay with Vijay for a couple of nights—his parents understood and had said that they were glad to help.

MAKING THINGS BETTER

Satisfied that Anita was safe for the time being, Dana explained what the agency would do to make things better. Several times throughout the conversation, Dana reminded Anita that everyone involved would be as sensitive as possible to her needs and feelings. She told Anita that she would be just a phone call away any time Anita had any questions or worries or just needed someone to talk to.

THE INVESTIGATION

Dana explained to Anita and Vijay that the next step would be an investigation of the situation. Social workers or other professionals trained in child welfare issues would talk with Anita and her parents. They might also talk to her neighbors, doctors, and teachers—maybe even to Vijay. They would probably visit her home to see for themselves what Anita's family life was like.

Anita asked if the investigators really needed to talk with her mother. It made her nervous that her mother would know that she had said these things about her. "Is there any way you can do this without talking to her?" she asked. Dana explained that it was important to talk to Anita's mother. Dana reminded Anita that any time she felt threatened, she could call.

Investigators would actually need to talk with her mother several times, Dana explained. They'd listen closely to her answers, especially if those answers seemed to change from one meeting to the next. They'd also check to see whether there had been any previous reports about her.

ASSESSMENT AND DECISION

"Here comes the tricky part," Dana said. "We are going to find a solution that will keep you safe, and if it is in any way possible, keep you and your mother together."

When Dana said that, Anita really became frightened. Dana made it sound as if there would be a few weeks of peace as the investigators kept a close eye on the family. But after that, if she and her mother still lived together, wouldn't things go back to the way they were, or be even worse? How could she and her mother ever live together without her being in danger of a beating?

Dana said, "I understand your concerns. Things will never go back to the way they have been. You and your mother—and maybe the whole family—will go for counseling. No one is going to leave you in your house with your mother until we are sure that it is safe."

TREATMENT AND COUNSELING

Psychological counseling is one of the most effective ways to end child abuse. Dana explained some of the ways in which counseling helps abusers:

▶ Individual and group counseling help abusers learn healthy ways to handle their anger and frustration.

▶ Family counseling, in which the whole family meets regularly with a counselor, enables the counselor to see how the family behaves together so that he or she can make suggestions for healthier behavior.

▶ Parenting classes teach parents how to discipline their children without violence.

▶ Self-help groups, such as Alcoholics Anonymous or Narcotics Anonymous, help abusers who have alcohol or drug problems overcome their addictions.

▶ A self-help group called Parents Anonymous helps parents who abuse, or might abuse, their children by offering these parents somewhere to turn when things become too difficult to handle alone.

Dana explained that once they understood more about what was going on in their home, Anita's mother

Counselors try to help abusers learn to handle their own problems. Meanwhile the family unit is supervised so that children are safe and secure.

and the rest of her family would participate in one or more of these programs.

IN THE MEANTIME

Anita asked how long all of this counseling would take. Dana admitted that she didn't know. "But while the counseling continues, we will do whatever we can to put your home back into order. If it's safe, we'll let your mother continue to live at home. If it's not safe, we may recommend that she move out for a while. But—and this is important—it's rare that a child abuser is forced to leave home forever. If she does leave for a while, we'll make sure that she comes back as soon as it's safe—and not before that."

No two cases of child abuse are the same. Anita's story is just one in millions. It does give you an idea of what happens when child abuse is reported, however. The key goals of child welfare agencies are:

▶ Immediate protection of the child

▶ Long-term protection of the child

▶ To bring the child's family together in a safe and productive way

TAKING FURTHER STEPS

What happens when the abuser can't or won't stop the abuse? Child welfare workers are not police officers. They can't force anyone to do anything. They can recommend that the abuser move out or go for counseling. But if the abuser refuses to follow those recommendations—or if the counseling doesn't work—the child may still be in danger. In that case, the child welfare workers will bring the matter to court.

The judge may order the abuser to stay away from the child. The judge may order that the abuser go to counseling or undergo treatment. If the abuser does not follow the judge's orders, the court can send him or her to jail. Child abuse is a crime, and judges have the authority to stop criminal activities.

If an abuser is unable or unwilling to change, even after counseling, there are laws to keep the abuser away from the family.

PUTTING THE FAMILY TOGETHER AGAIN

THE EFFECTS OF ABUSE

Tyrone was an abused child. He spent most of his childhood bruised, cut, and with broken bones. When he grew older and moved out of his home, those physical injuries healed.

Stuart wasn't as lucky as Tyrone was. He was also abused, but as a result, he suffered permanent hearing loss. The physical effects of his abuse will last forever.

Billie was neglected as a child. Now that she's grown up, she still suffers from malnutrition and breathing problems.

Tyrone, Stuart, and Billie share some other traits also. As a result of the abuse and neglect they endured as children, they have emotional, learning, and behavioral problems.

Emotional Problems

Children who are hurt by family members—or by others who are close to them—have a lot of conflicting feelings to deal with. Someone they love, who loves them, is attacking them or neglecting them. It's hard to understand such love and such scary behavior at the same time.

Children in abusive homes may feel depressed, afraid, anxious, sad, or guilty. They often have sleeping or eating problems. Victims of childhood sexual abuse generally have even more serious problems. They carry feelings of shame. They may feel dirty and may have difficulty trusting other people. Children who are forced into sexual activity may have problems when they become adults. They often find it difficult to have healthy relationships.

Learning Problems

It's hard to pay attention in school when things are difficult at home. If you're thinking about the abuse, or if you don't have the care and love you need, you can't concentrate on your schoolwork. Some abused children feel so unhappy that they don't make it to school at all.

Behavioral Problems

Wallace was sexually abused by his uncle. He hated it, but didn't know how to stop it. So he took his anger out in dangerous ways. He mistreated his younger brother. He misbehaved in class. And he abused himself. He began to use alcohol and other drugs. He dropped out of school. In time, he ran away from home.

WHAT COUNSELING IS LIKE

Because of all the emotional, learning, and behavioral problems that abused children face, counseling is very important. Counseling takes some time and hard work, but it does help. It helps children understand what

Victims of abuse need someone strong and positive to talk to. Young people who run away often remain scared and alone with their bad feelings.

they have experienced. It helps them work out any bad feelings and conflicting thoughts they may have. It gives children a safe place to talk and a place to pay attention to some very difficult emotions and fears. It may also stop the cycle of abuse from continuing when they have children. It gives them a chance to have what everyone deserves: a healthy, strong, and productive future.

WHERE TO GO FROM HERE

We've tried to make it clear that if you are abused, you are not alone. There are many other victims just like you or anyone else you know. But all too many victims hide behind shame and guilt, allowing their abusers to escape without restraint or rehabilitation. Don't let them take advantage of you a moment longer. Ask for help now—you deserve it and are owed it!

emotional abuse: Saying or doing something on purpose to make someone feel bad.

emotional neglect: Ignoring the emotional needs of a person, such as the need for love and attention.

family counseling: Family members meet regularly with a counselor. The counselor observes how the family members interact and offers suggestions for improving the interactions.

genitals: External sexual organs.

group counseling: A group of people who have a similar problem meets regularly with a counselor. Group members share their experiences and find solutions to their problems under the guidance of the counselor.

incest: Sexual intercourse between family members who are so closely related that they are forbidden by law to marry.

individual counseling: A person meets regularly with a counselor to talk about problems and feelings. Together they figure out ways to help the person feel better.

neglect: Ignore the physical care or safety of someone.

physical abuse: Hitting, slapping, pushing, biting, shaking, burning, or in other ways causing intentional physical injury to a person.

self-help group: Group of people who meet regularly to share their experiences and offer support to one another.

sexual abuse: Touching or using a person in a sexual way; forcing a person to have sexual intercourse.

sexual intercourse: The sexual act in which the male's penis enters the female's vagina.

WHERE TO GO FOR HELP

There are many national organizations that can help you learn more about child neglect and abuse. Several of them are listed below. Each of these groups can put you in touch with a counselor or other person who can answer your questions and send you booklets, brochures, and other information.

Your best bet is to call a local organization. Local groups can find you the help you need right away. To find these groups, look in your telephone book under the words "child abuse," "children's protective services," or "family services." You can also call a local health center or public health department, a social services agency, or the police.

American Humane Association
Children's Division
63 Inverness Drive E.
Englewood, CO 80112
1-303-792-9900

Canadian Society for the
Prevention of Cruelty
to Children
25 Spadina Road
Toronto, ON M5R 2S9
1-416-921-3151

Childhelp USA
P.O. Box 4175
Woodland Hills, CA 91370
1-800-422-4453
1-800-222-4453 (TDD)

Kids Help Phone
100-2 Bloor Street W.
P.O. Box 513
Toronto, ON M4W 3E2
1-800-668-6868

National Coalition Against
Domestic Violence
P.O. Box 18749
Denver, CO 80218-0749
1-303-839-1852

National Committee for
Prevention of Child Abuse
332 S. Michigan Avenue,
Suite 1600
Chicago, IL 60604
1-800-835-2671

National Council on Child
Abuse and Family Violence
1155 Connecticut Avenue, NW
Washington, DC 20036
1-800-222-2000

Oxfam International
156 George Street
Fitzroy, Victoria 3065
Australia

Books

Ackerman, Robert J., and Dee Graham. *Too Old to Cry.* TAB Books, 1990.

Berger, Gilda. *Violence and the Family.* Franklin Watts, 1990.

Gilbert, Sara. *Get Help: Solving the Problems in Your Life.* Morrow Junior Books, 1989.

Goldentyer, Debra. *Family Violence.* Raintree Steck-Vaughn, 1995.

Greenberg, Keith. *Family Abuse: Why Do People Hurt Each Other?* Twenty-First Century, 1994.

Haskins, James. *The Child Abuse Help Book.* Addison-Wesley, 1982.

Hyde, Margaret O. *Know About Abuse.* Walker and Company, 1992.

Ito, Tom. *Child Abuse.* Lucent, 1995.

Landau, Elaine. *Child Abuse: An American Epidemic.* Julian Messner, 1990.

Mufson, Susan, and Rachel Kranz. *Straight Talk About Child Abuse.* Dell, 1993.

Park, Angela. *Child Abuse.* Aladdin, 1988.

Rench, Janice E. *Family Violence.* Lerner, 1992.

INDEX